Children's Ministry Guides

Children's Ministry has a commitment to provide the resources and training needed to help busy children's workers develop their ability to evangelize and disciple the children in their community.

Children's Ministry Guides are short, easy-to-read books offering practical insight into key areas of children's ministry. They compliment the other resources and training opportunities available from Children's Ministry including:

- conferences
- training days
- distance learning courses
- undated, activity-based, Bible-centred teaching programme
- books of ready-to-use ideas
- books of opinion and wisdom from children's ministry practitioners
- cds and music books of children's praise songs
- supporting resources

For more details about the Children's Ministry range of resources visit www.childrensministry.co.uk or call 01323 437748.

GW00602014

Other titles in the series:

Fun and Games
for
Active Learning

JENNY BROWN
with
Ruth Alliston, Cathy Kyte,
Sue Price and Andy Back

Series edited by Sue Price

EASTBOURNE

ISBN 1 - 84291 - 091 - 4

Published by
KINGSWAY COMMUNICATIONS LTD,
Lottbridge Drove, Eastbourne, BN23 6NT, UK.
Cover design and book production for the publishers by
Bookprint Creative Services, P.O. Box 827, BN21 3YJ, England.
Printed in Great Britain.

In memory of my inspirational grandmother,
Marie Hawthorne,
a fun, lively and enthusiastic woman of God
and sportswoman until her final years.

Contents

Acknowledgements

I feel privileged to be part of the innovative, forward-thinking Children's Ministry team at Kingsway. Thank you to the whole team – firstly, for taking on a teacher and athlete and helping her to write; secondly, for being such fun to work with; and, thirdly, for coping with my hyperactive lifestyle!

I am very grateful to Sue Price for allowing me the flexible hours that have enabled me to pursue a running career alongside my job. Special mention to Andy Back, a talented writer, co-worker and great friend who has taught me so much. We are completely different in almost every way but normally manage to complement each other rather than argue. Thanks, Andy!

God has also been fantastic in bringing my husband, Roland, and myself to Kings Church, Eastbourne. Thank you to Kings, and especially Janet Johnston, for allowing me to try out new ideas, for giving me much wise advice and for being an inspiration to work with. Roland supports me brilliantly in everything I do whilst keeping my feet on the ground. Recently this has included reading many drafts of this book. Thank you, Ro!

I'd also like to gratefully acknowledge the help I've received from Stuart Weir and Jill Ireland of Christians In Sport, particularly concerning the chapter Gods, Games and Church. Finally, I'd like to thank my Dad, John Hawthorne, biologist and athletics coach, who checked the scientific parts of this book, who encouraged me to have an active childhood, and who has supported me so magnificently ever since we found out I could run round fields faster than most!

Introduction

This book has been written for all who love children and wish to help them learn, grow and develop into the person God made them to be, fulfilling their potential and living life in abundance. Although our focus is on Christian education – Bible teaching, discipleship and evangelism – much here can be applied to all areas of education and so the hope is that anyone involved in teaching any subject will be able to gain something from what they read.

The central theme of this book is that movement is good for learning. Within its pages you can:

- Explore how God has designed our bodies to move and how he encourages us to learn through action;
- Enhance your understanding of why all children will benefit from movement activities;
- Consider a variety of practical examples of fun-filled activities for children of all ages that will help you to incorporate movement into your teaching and discipleship;

- Find ideas for using games and sport in evangelism to help you to connect with energetic young followers of the 'sporting gods'.

Part of the motivation for writing this book comes from my own experiences. As a very active child, I did not particularly enjoy our rather static Sunday school lessons. From the age of ten, when I took up athletics, sport gradually consumed more and more of my time and winning races certainly seemed more exciting than sitting in church. Jesus seemed irrelevant to me. However, as a student I realized that sport was not a suitable foundation on which to build my life and I became a Christian during my first year away from home. Recently, time spent with top athletes as part of the Great Britain Athletics Team has reinforced my view that many active and sports-minded people are not uninterested in Jesus but, as was my experience in my teens, have never heard about him in a way that connects with their lives.

Over the last twelve years, the opportunities God has given me through my Sports Science studies, a spell as a primary teacher, a variety of work with children in several local churches and, most recently, a fascinating and enjoyable period writing for Children's Ministry, have taught me a great deal about children, the Bible and education. I have plenty more to learn, but through this book I am pleased to be able to share the knowledge I have gained concerning how children can learn about Jesus and get to know him through games and physical activity.

When most people think of children learning they tend to imagine classrooms filled with tables and chairs. Most education normally involves sitting still, listening, writing, drawing and talking. We have moved on a good deal since the first schools and Sunday Schools with their often cramped classrooms, rote learning and memorization. The stages of children's development are now recognized and education does not try to force children to become little adults before their time. However, most education does not involve a lot of movement after the ages of four or five.

Even in ancient Greek times play was recognized as valuable and for centuries various educationalists have advocated active learning as worthwhile. During the last 100 years, one type of education that has grown is Montessori's educational method, promoting an environment of structured activity choice. More recently, Gardner's theory of multiple intelligences has promoted the use of a variety of styles of teaching and learning for all ages, including learning through movement.

Current educational research is pointing towards a more active style of learning; physical activity has been shown to be beneficial to brain development and learning, as well as to our general physical and mental health. There is a minimum level of physical activity necessary for a healthy body and brain, and the declining level of activity amongst all sections of the population, especially children, gives cause for concern.

It is also clear that some children need to move more than is often considered acceptable in order to learn effectively – the bodily- or tactile-kinesthetic learners. When asked to sit still these are the ones that are likely to fiddle, fidget, rock on their chair or roll around the floor. Some children who are labelled as having special educational needs may be those who need to learn in a different way. Research tells us that all children will benefit from the incorporation of more movement into their education, but for these children it is essential if they are to succeed in learning. Their intelligence and talent may not be evident in traditional paper and pencil tasks that rely on auditory and visual skills, but in the arts, sport and practical activities, which may actually be more useful in adulthood.

I can think of several children I taught in my primary school classes who flourished when given the opportunity to break away from pencil and paper tasks – Jamie, who needed to write in sand to learn to spell, and speak rather than write stories and reports; Antony who excelled in sport and drama but found it hard to sit still; Jack, who liked to tell everyone his latest ideas and loved to experiment. It is tragic that so many children like these consider themselves to be failures because their learning style is not catered for in mainstream education.

Planning and implementing movement activities can seem a hard task. Many of us will feel that it is far easier to have all the children sitting down, quietly listening, reading, writing and colouring. Some of us will feel rather inadequate ourselves when it comes to physical activity. Just as not everyone enjoys and learns from sitting still, not everyone enjoys action songs, running about, dance, drama and mad games! Your natural learning and teaching style is very unlikely to suit all the children in your group. However, you can still organize lively activities if you are unable or unwilling to take part yourself. It will be more fun for the children if you do join in, but don't starve the children of movement if your physical health or fear of embarrassment make this difficult. You may have concerns about involving children who dislike activity or have special needs that limit their participation. Chapter 5 includes some advice for you. Some people may worry about discipline and safety issues with more lively activities. Refer to the Appendix for help in these areas.

In this book the focus is on using games, sports and action in your teaching. Of course, active learning encompasses far more. For further ideas, see the *Children's Ministry Teaching Programme* which uses drama, dance, action songs, arts and crafts and more to help children learn from the Bible in a contemporary, lively way. *The Children's Ministry Guide to Using Dance and Drama* by Ruth Alliston will provide you with useful background information and a range of ideas for using these teaching methods.

There are many reasons why you may read this book. Perhaps you will identify with one or more of these sentiments:

- I have previously seen games and action as unnecessary 'just for fun' activities.
- I enjoy games and action and I am looking for more ideas.
- I have lively children in my group.
- I have found this type of activity difficult to manage in the past.
- I have been asked to lead an activity and don't know where to start.
- I need to introduce more fun to my sessions – I'm afraid the children find them boring.

Whatever your reasons, I hope what you read here, and in the other books in this series, will renew your enthusiasm and provide you with new ideas as you teach and disciple the children in your care. I pray that you will also be encouraged to reach out to other active children in your area who never knew learning about Jesus could be such fun!

Jenny Brown, Eastbourne, January 2003

1. Made to Move

God has designed us to move. We are made in the image of an active God and our bodies are intricately designed with muscles, tendons and ligaments and cardiovascular, digestive and nervous systems so that we can perform a mind-blowing variety of gross (running, jumping, climbing) and fine (writing, painting, facial expressions) motor movements.

God of action

God is a God of action. At creation, the Spirit of God hovered over the waters and God's intentions became actions as he made light, darkness, seas, sky, land, plants, stars, planets and animals. God expresses himself through action. Working through man and through nature, God has acted throughout history to accomplish his purposes.

To human beings, whose primary means of communication is through sight, sound and movement, God speaks through his creation (Romans 1:20) and supremely, through the words and actions of his Son:

The Word became flesh and made his dwelling among us.
(John 1:14)

That which was from the beginning, that which we have heard, which we have seen with our eyes, which we have looked at and our hands have touched – this we proclaim ... (1 John 1:1)

Human beings too must express themselves through action. Some sort of physical action is needed for any thought to be expressed. Facial expressions and body position show emotion. Muscular movements are needed to speak. To perform any action our brains must engage our body.

If we go back to Adam and Eve and prehistoric times, it is obvious to see that a good deal of physical activity was necessary for survival. In both hunter-gatherer and early farming communities, life revolved around having sufficient food and water and that meant physical work to produce, catch or collect it.

Throughout history children's play and education has consisted, at least in part, of copying the adults. Children in these ancient cultures must have experienced a very active style of play and education from a very early age.

As still happens in many rural cultures in the developing world, children would have begun to assist with food gathering and animal rearing as young as five or six. In fact, throughout biblical times, ordinary daily life involved relatively high levels of physical activity for both adults and children.

Physical activity is good

In simple health terms, physical activity is good. Physical activity increases both length and quality of life and can reduce or protect against cardiovascular disease, cancer, Type 2 diabetes and osteoporosis. Bones and muscles are strengthened. Physical activity increases muscle fibre and nerve cell growth and can improve strength, speed, endurance, flexibility and co-ordination.

Nowadays, increasing television viewing, Internet usage and computer game playing mean that both children and adults lead a more sedentary lifestyle compared to previous generations. One in four children watches at least four hours of television a day. Over 70 per cent of children in Britain have televisions and videos in their bedroom.[1] Few children walk to school and parents are understandably hesitant to allow their children to play outside without supervision.

Our bodies are made to move and lack of activity can have the following consequences:

Heart disease

Physically inactive people in Great Britain have about double the risk of heart attack and an increased risk of stroke compared to those who are moderately to vigorously active. Seven out of ten adults in the UK do not take enough regular exercise to protect their health. Habits formed in childhood tend to continue into adult life so lifestyle choices early in life promote good health in adulthood.

The Health Education Authority recommends that children and young people should aim to participate in activity of at least moderate intensity for one hour everyday.[2] Physical activity helps improve blood cholesterol levels, helps to prevent blood clotting, helps to lower high blood pressure and prevents high blood pressure from developing.

Obesity

One in ten children starting primary school in Britain is classed as substantially overweight and this figure rises to fifteen per cent of school leavers. Although some people naturally put on weight more easily than others, fast foods and lack of exercise are major and more significant factors.[3] Obesity, rather than being an illness, is actually a natural physiological response to the way we now live.

Newspaper headlines are warning of an obesity epidemic amongst our children and teenagers. The British Association for the Advancement of Science predicts that many parents will outlive their children due to the health problems suffered by their children as a result of obesity.[4]

Impaired sensory development

If a child remains still for long periods of time, for example while watching television, his sensory development may be impaired. In young children, the area of the brain controlling balance and the co-ordination of vision with movement is not likely to develop properly (see Under 5's section).

Sight and hearing are the main senses used while watching television, while the other senses are hardly used. Experiences of touch, warmth, movement, sight, sound, taste, smell are vital to the development of the central nervous system. Children who are active will be developing their senses far better than those watching television will. As they naturally mimic the activities of adults – such as in pretend games involving 'cooking', 'gardening', 'cleaning', 'shopping', 'building', 'driving', etc. – and play active games, they are unconsciously developing their bodies and minds ready for further learning and for the adult world.

Restricted emotional development

Children enjoy active games. Apart from being fun in themselves, physical activities, especially activities involving walking, running, swimming, dancing and cycling, release chemicals which increase a person's sense of well-being and reduce anxiety and stress. In addition, self-esteem can rise as children improve in their ability to control their body and master new skills.

Diminished social development

Playing games together helps children learn to co-operate and work as a team. Friendships are built through games that involve interaction. Creativity is stimulated. Children's self-discipline can grow as they set rules for games themselves or adhere to standard rules and see that there must be organisation and discipline for a game to work. Winning and losing are part of many games and children develop strategies for coping with successes and disappointments in life. Physical activity can be a safe outlet for aggression.

Recent studies have demonstrated the positive social effects of physical activity in children and young people. For example, a break time walking programme for primary age children in the USA, with healthy snacks and T-shirts as incentives to take part, led to improved discipline. The year before the programme, over one hundred serious playground discipline problems were reported, but during the walking programme there were only two.

For further details and other examples see *Learning with the Body in Mind*, by Eric Jensen, an expert in brain-based learning.[5]

Summary

God has designed us to move. If we don't take sufficient exercise, our minds and bodies will suffer. This alone is a good reason for incorporating movement into children's activities and promoting an active lifestyle.

In addition to the health implications of exercise, or the lack of it, learning improves with physical activity. Some children need to move in order to learn well. Scientific research tells us all children will benefit from active learning because movement helps to anchor new information in the memory.

Chapter 2 gives a brief overview of the science behind learning through movement. If you would prefer to go straight to the practical sections of the book, don't feel you have to read all the scientific information. You may also wish to skip the historical aspects covered in Chapter 3. However, those chapters do provide background reasoning for all that follows and so I hope you will return to them at a later date to gain a more thorough understanding of why your children need to move.

Footnotes

1   Clouder, Christopher, Jenkinson, Sally, and Large, Martin. (ed.) *'Out of the Box'* in *The Future of Childhood.* Hawthorne Press, UK, 2000.

2   British Heart Foundation, *Get Kids on the Go!* British Heart Foundation, 2000. p3.

3   British Association for the Advancement of Science web site www.britas-soc.org.uk

4   Daily Telegraph, Tuesday September 10th 2002.

5   Jensen, Eric. *Learning with the Body in Mind – The Scientific Basis for Energizers, Movement, Play, Games, and Physical Education.* The Brain Store, Inc., San Diego, CA, USA, 2000. pp80-85.

2. Active Learning

When God wanted his people to remember something important he often commanded action. For example:

- The Laws and commandments were to be taught in all sorts of ways:

  Fix these words of mine in your hearts and minds; tie them as symbols on your hands and bind them on your foreheads. Teach them to your children, talking about them when you sit at home and when you walk along the road, when you lie down and when you get up. Write them on the doorframes of your houses and on your gates... (Deuteronomy 11:18-20)

- The deliverance from Egypt was to be remembered through the Passover festival (Leviticus 23:4-8).
- The festival of Firstfruits was to be celebrated to give thanks for God's provision (Leviticus 23:9-14).

- The feast of Weeks or Pentecost was ordained to thank God for the harvest (Leviticus 23:15-21).
- The festival of Tabernacles was to be a time to remember the journey from Egypt to Canaan (Leviticus 23:33-36).
- The feast of Purim was instigated to remember the people's deliverance at the time of Esther (Esther 9:18-32).
- Stones were often moved into certain positions to remind the people of significant events, for example, the crossing of the Jordan:

Each of you is to take up a stone on his shoulder ... to serve as a sign among you. In the future, when your children ask you, 'What do these stones mean?' tell them that the flow of the Jordan was cut off before the ark of the covenant of the Lord.... These stones are to be a memorial to the people of Israel for ever. (Joshua 4:4-7)

- Jesus told his disciples to remember his sacrificial death on the cross by eating bread and drinking wine.

This is my body given for you; do this in remembrance of me. (Luke 22:17:20)

Repentance and new life is demonstrated through baptism. (Matthew 28:19)

Interestingly, but not surprisingly, recent research proves that hearing or seeing combined with movement is one of the best ways to learn.

Movement is integral to learning

The human body with its vast networks of nerves, blood vessels and muscles is designed to move. It is now accepted that the body and mind cannot be thought of as two separate entities.

To understand the mind-body connection we need a basic understanding of how the central nervous system (brain and spinal cord), nerves and muscles interact.

Mind-body interaction

Any movement, however small, requires interaction between the central nervous system (CNS) made up of the brain and spinal cord, and the nerves and muscles. Let us imagine, for example, that Bethany, ten, wishes to put her hand up in order to answer a question during a quiz:

- Firstly, her brain must know the starting position of her arm. Receptors found in her joints, tendons, muscles, skin, connective tissues and vestibular system (the balance sensing mechanism positioned in the inner ear), constantly send messages to her brain via nerves (called *sensory neurones*) allowing it to know the position of her entire body. Bethany will also be visually aware of the position of her arm, with nerves sending messages to her brain from her eyes.

- Her brain receives the messages and the information is processed through pathways of brain cells (*intermediate neurones*) situated in the areas (or *lobes*) of the brain responsible for that part of her body.

- Her brain sends messages to her arm muscles via nerves called *motor neurones* to initiate movement.

- As her arm is moving, this cycle from receptors through

sensory neurones to the CNS and back via motor neurones to the muscles continues constantly so that her brain knows the position of her arm at all times and can continue moving it or stop the movement when necessary.

All this must happen in a split second so that Bethany can get her hand up quickly and have a chance of being chosen to answer the question.

Thought and movement are intimately connected. The brain cannot express a single thought without movement, be that movement of the eye muscles in order to look in a certain direction, muscles of speech in order to talk, or the majority of the muscles of the body in order to run.

Similarly, information about the environment, received by the body, must go to the brain in order for any sense to be made of it. We have already mentioned receptors which sense position, movement and pressure. We also possess temperature receptors, taste receptors, smell receptors, light receptors and sound receptors. All these receptors send messages to our brains via nerves to enable us to sense our environment and our relationship to it.

How learning happens

When we learn something new, the connections in our brains change. With new experiences, the networks of inter-mediate neurones are moulded into a different shape with better properties. New patterns and pathways form.

Neurones network by forming many extensions (called *dendrites*) that enable the neurone to communicate with many other neurones. Most pathways develop through stimulation and experience – as sensory stimuli are received and the brain sends out messages, growth of dendrites between neurones in the brain is stimulated. If a stimulus and action is repeated then pathways develop and learning occurs.

The ability of the brain to adapt to the environment is greatest in young children. A baby initially learns basic movements such as holding up his head and grasping objects. My nephew, Joshua, at a few months old, has reached this stage.

As a child responds to a new stimulus or a more difficult demand, the number of connections in the brain increases and new pathways form. Sophie, at three, has moved from merely holding objects to being able to manipulate them. The pathway enabling her to hold something has adapted to enable her to exhibit more control. Rachel, at five, has, through practice, increased the dendritic connections in her brain so that she is able to write. Philip, approaching eight, has well-developed hand-eye co-ordination and can play squash. This involves many inter-related pathways so that he can run, dodge and hit the ball successfully. Dendritic connections are continually developed as he practices each week.

With age, it becomes more difficult for the brain to adapt and form new pathways. I would find it difficult to learn to play squash and could be beaten by Philip despite being aerobically fitter and physically stronger through other athletic training.

Other learning, e.g. academic-type learning, happens in a similar way. Pathways of intermediate neurones in the relevant brain areas receive new information via the senses, normally ears and/or eyes. Previous knowledge is stored in these pathways and these are updated through changing dendritic connections as the new information is processed. When Hannah, ten, has a new list of spellings to learn, she already possesses a good deal of knowledge about how words are formed. New dendritic connections form as she updates her spelling knowledge with the new words. She will probably practise writing and speaking the sequence of letters for each word because, although she is unaware of it, the movement involved will increase dendritic connections and form stronger pathways. Movement helps her to learn. Similarly, Shaun, twelve, as he takes part in a role-play exercise based on a Bible passage he's just heard, will be increasing the connections in his brain as he talks and moves, bringing about learning.

The movement-learning connection

So, thought and movement are intimately connected. The body is totally reliant on the brain in order to sense the environment. The brain can only express a thought via the body. As the environment, body and brain interact, neuronal connections increase, learning occurs, and our understanding, memory and muscular control improve.

Practically speaking:

- Practising a certain movement, for example, a football skill or handwriting, will lead to improvements in that skill.
- Writing, drawing, speaking or acting out an item or set of information to be learned will enhance memory by strengthening neural pathways.

Children need to do something with information they receive. For some, writing, drawing or talking about it will be sufficient, but for many, particularly young children, incorporating more movement into their education will be necessary.

Some children learn well through movement

The theory of multiple intelligences developed by Howard Gardner[1] suggests that intelligence can be classified in eight different ways: linguistic, logical-mathematical, spatial, bodily-kinesthetic (also termed tactile-kinesthetic), musical, interpersonal, intrapersonal and naturalist. Children tend to have strengths in one or more intelligences and will learn best when operating in this area.

Intelligence preference	Preferred method of learning
Linguistic	words – visual or auditory
Logical-mathematical	logical patterns, numbers and reasoning
Spatial	pictures and images, diagrams, charts
Bodily-kinesthetic	tactile and bodily sensations, movement, making things
Musical	melody and rhythm
Interpersonal	social interaction, co-operative learning, discussions
Intrapersonal	introspection, individual work
Naturalist	nature experiences, animals, plants, environment

However, all children possess the eight intelligences in varying degrees and so can benefit from the full spectrum of activities and experiences.

In this book, we will focus on the tactile/bodily-kinesthetic intelligence and how children learn through movement. Marlene LeFever, in *Learning Styles*, also identifies the bodily-kinesthetic intelligence as one of the main ways in which children learn.[2]

All young children are tactile-kinesthetic learners – they learn by moving. In their first years at school, some children change towards a visual learning preference – they learn best from what they see. By the time they reach secondary education, some will have become auditory learners, learning best from what they hear. Many people remain tactile-kinesthetic learners, particularly boys, while some do not have a strong preference in the way that they learn. Hence, if we use tactile-kinesthetic teaching methods, we will be matching the learning style of a large proportion of the children we teach. If our children are predominantly pre-school or boys then this teaching style should be the dominant one. Look out for children who fidget when you are hoping they will sit still, look and listen – they will almost certainly exhibit a strong preference for tactile-kinesthetic learning. They will be the sort of child who likes to run, jump, play sport, build, touch everything they see, make crafts, etc.

EXAMPLE: BODILY-KINESTHETIC TEACHING IN ACTION
A middle school in northern Virginia, believing in the concept of learning through movement, experimented with this method in 1998-9. The majority of the pupils, when questioned, identified Gardner's bodily-kinesthetic intelligence as their most highly developed intelligence and reported that they were motivated by a hands-on learning approach. Below are a few examples of how subjects were

taught in a bodily-kinesthetic style:

- In mathematics, pupils learned about shapes and angles by working in the gym creating human shapes and moving patterns set to music.
- In science, pupils studied language in orang-utans and then made up their own language using movements.
- In poetry, pupils used the rhythm of a poem in the gym.
- Physical education and mathematics were combined when students recorded heart rates and created graphs.

Pupils felt they were learning more using these methods and the school's academic test results improved.[3]

Exercise increases learning

Recent research with rats suggests that a good level of everyday exercise increases their capacity to learn. It is believed that the results achieved with rats will also hold true in humans. Initial studies with older adults have borne out these results. Studies have shown that:

- Regular aerobic exercise improves blood flow and oxygen supply to the brain.[4, 5]
- Regular aerobic exercise causes brain cells to be supplied with more neurotrophins, natural substances that enhance cell growth and slow cell death.[6]
- Exercise that involves complex skills (obstacle courses were used with rats) stimulates brain cell growth and increases levels of neurotransmitters, substances that enable brain cells to communicate.[7]

So, according to these results, it would be expected that in addition to the general health benefits outlined in Chapter 1, children's learning capacity will be improved with regular exercise.

Summary

The tactile-kinesthetic learning style is not the preference of every child, but every child will benefit from movement activities, due to the strengthening of pathways in the brain that occurs and the benefits of exercise to the brain and body. God has designed us to learn through movement so let's make sure we include plenty of active games and learning activities into our teaching sessions.

The church has not always been positive towards games, sport and fun and there is still some debate today about how games and sport fit in with church and Christian life. Sport certainly competes for the attention of both children and adults on Sundays and throughout the week. We will consider these issues briefly in Chapter 3.

Footnotes

1   Armstrong, Thomas. *Multiple Intelligences: Seven Ways to Approach Curriculum.* www.thomasarmstrong.com/articles

2   LeFever, Marlene. *Learning Styles: Reaching everyone God gave you to teach.* Kingsway Publications, UK, 1998. pp. 147-164.

3   Lancaster, E. and Rikard, G Linda. *Across the Curriculum Learning Through Movement.* Middle School Journal, January 2002.

4   Isaacs, K.R. et al. *Exercise and the brain: Angiogenesis in the adult rat cerebellum after vigorous physical activity and motor skill learning.* J Cereb Blood Flow Metab 1992 Jan; 12(1):110-119.

5   Beckman Institute, Annual Report 2000. Web site: www.beckman.uiuc.

6   Brinks, Susan. *Smart Moves.* US News and World Report Archive, May 15, 1995. Web site: www.usnews.com.

7   van Praag, H. et al. *Neural Consequences of Environmental Enrichment,* Nature Reviews Neuroscience 1, 191-198 (2000). Web site: www.nature.com.

3. Gods, Games and Church

In ancient times, religious rituals and ceremonies could be very physically energetic, and it was in this context that games, dances and physical challenges would be performed. Indeed, this is still the case in some cultures today.

In New Testament times, Jewish culture would not have approved of sport with its links with pagan rituals, the worship of champions and accompanying worldly festivities. Christians then and now would agree with this to some extent.

However, biblical writers did not condemn sport and games and a positive attitude to sport can be biblically justified (see below). Since the first century, the church has had a stormy relationship with games and sports, sometimes promoting physical activity and sometimes trying to divorce herself from it. What follows is a series of snap shots of the church and her relationship with sport and games.

For further details, refer to *What the Book says about Sport*, an excellent paperback by Stuart Weir of Christians in Sport.

New Testament references to sport and games

In the New Testament we find Paul and others using the language of sport to help the early church to understand the Christian life. They took their examples from the Greek and Roman sport of the day. Weir writes, 'Just as Jesus often expressed spiritual truth in the rural language that the country folk of Judea would understand – the lost sheep, the sower, the wheat and the weeds, and so on – so Paul, writing to people with a Greek mindset, used the language of the games.'[1]

Greek sport and games

In ancient Greece, dancing and other rituals involving physical activity were still associated with religious belief and mythology, as was the case in earlier times. Olympia became the site of the Olympic games, due to its importance in Greek myths – there was a strong link between religion and physical prowess. As nowadays, the games were held every four years, although there were no measurements or record keeping and it was certainly not a world-wide competition.

On the whole, sports were designed for young men and were based on the skills of a warrior – chariot racing, wrestling, boxing, throwing discus and javelin, running, long jumping and archery. Athletes became the champions of society – young, male and wealthy. Corinth was the host of the Isthmian Games, second only in importance to the Olympics and of a similar nature.

Roman sport and games

The Romans used sports and games both for warrior training and for entertainment. They adapted Greek ideas so

that the games, contests and races were more useful for
soldiers and more suitable as spectator sports. Many of the
contests were extremely violent – boxing, bear-baiting, bull-
baiting and animal fights were popular. Gladiators fought to
the death and 'troublesome' members of society, generally
criminals and Christians, were forced to fight lions, tigers
and panthers. Chariot races were common and the most
popular spectator sport. Slaves were often used as chario-
teers. The Roman leaders saw spectator 'sports' events as a
useful way to entertain the 'masses' who, with free time,
could have become troublesome. Women were seldom
involved in actual contests but were keen spectators.

The Roman Games (*Ludi Romani*) were a major religious
festival lasting up to six weeks with chariot races and athletic competitions. There were many public holidays in Roman
times and so there was also time for informal games. Ball
games were popular, including various types of catching
games, a type of soccer, hockey and Harpastum, a game a
little like rugby.

Biblical examples
Corinth hosted the Isthmian Games every three years.
Every competitor had to go into strict training for ten
months. Successful athletes would win a pine wreath. Here
is part of one of Paul's letters to the Corinthians:

> Do you not know that in a race all the runners run, but only one
> gets the prize? Everyone who competes in the games goes into
> strict training. They do it to get a crown that will not last; but we do
> it to get a crown that will last for ever. Therefore, I do not run like
> a man running aimlessly; I do not fight like a man beating the air.

No, I beat my body and make it my slave so that after I have preached to others, I myself will not be disqualified for the prize. (1 Corinthians 9:24-27)

Other similar passages include Galatians 5:7; 1 Timothy 4:7-8; 2 Timothy 2:5; and Hebrews 12:1-3.

The church and sport in Britain

In Medieval Europe, sports and games were again used both as military training and as a form of entertainment but now there was more emphasis on general participation.

By Norman times, there was no specific link between sport and games and religion, although the church encouraged games in many areas. The peasant classes played folk games and these became a feature of village life as priests encouraged games by opening church grounds on holidays and Sunday afternoons.

The Reformation

The Protestant Reformation brought negative attitudes to sport and games. For the first time we see a definite separation between sports and religion. From the early 1500s to the late 1600s English Puritans tried to eliminate or control leisure activities. They believed that work, worship and family were life's priorities and that sport and games, and particularly the partying, drinking and fun that went with them, were an unnecessary and ungodly distraction. Public games played on the Sabbath by the peasant class were easily curtailed but activities such as horse racing, tennis, bowling and hunting took place on the private property of the wealthy and so were harder to limit.

However, in the early 1600s the monarchy began to support festivals and public games and sports. *The King's Book of Sports*, which said that ministers should not discourage games, was issued by King James I and reissued by Charles I.

The Industrial Revolution

Starting in the middle of the 18th century, this changed work and community life dramatically. Factories and mass production meant that workers, including many children, had little free time. Days were long and tiring and the cities that grew up had few open spaces. In addition, ministers discouraged play, especially on Sundays.

During the 19th century there began to be concerns over the health of workers in factories and cities. Weak, sickly people could not work well so there was a call for open spaces and healthy exercise such as callisthenics, gymnastics and outdoor exercise. The Open Spaces Act was passed by parliament in 1906.

The doctrine of 'muscular Christianity' became influential during the 19th century.

Simply defined, this is 'manly' Christianity. Supporters were reacting against the more feminine influence in churches at the time. They believed in physical exertion, comradeship and determination and emphasized manliness, morality, health and patriotism.[2] The YMCA in England, founded in 1844, wanted people to see that exercise and sports were not anti-Christian.

Links between the environment and behaviour began to be understood and people saw that sport and games could be useful. Games weren't just for fun but could contribute to economic and social progress. Sports could change behaviour and build character, unity and national loyalty. Team sports were seen as useful for 'taming' lower class males.

Victorian times

During the second half of Victoria's reign most people had more money and more leisure time. Ordinary workers had time for sports and hobbies. Spectating was a popular pastime. Formally organized competitive sports began to be established with clubs, associations and championships being set up.

Physical education became a recognized school subject in Britain in 1893. By the beginning of the 20th century PE was widely taught in schools and a training college for PE teachers was established. Despite this being a positive initiative, the period marked the beginning of a slide from mass participation to mass spectating, although this was not really significant for another 50 years.

By the turn of the century the church again tended to shy away from sport, focusing on the negatives of Sunday competitions, the associated drinking and gambling, and the risk of injury.

Sport as a religion

More clubs, associations and championships were set up during the 20th century. Rather than being part of religious expression as in the ancient past, they almost became religions in themselves. Huge numbers of people will now go to a sports event rather than attend church on a Sunday. Sports players and supporters have their own special places, celebrations and dress codes. Sport dominates many people's lives.

Sport-related industries have grown up, sponsorship of successful sports teams and individuals has become common, and technology associated with sport has increased rapidly. Televised sport has a huge audience. Television watching and the rise of computer-based activities have probably been largely responsible for a fall in participation in informal sports and active games.

Certain Christian sports people, such as the Scottish sprinter, Eric Liddell of *Chariots of Fire* fame, have shone out amidst this idolization of sport, demonstrating that God comes first in their lives. Through their words and lifestyle Christian sports people aim to worship God as they train and compete. I know from personal experience that seeking to train and compete whilst keeping Jesus central is a hard task but an important way in which Christians can show 'the way, the truth and the life' to sports followers.

Organisations such as Christians in Sport (established in 1980) have been formed to reach the world of sport for Christ and to promote a Christian presence in sport. They seek to support Christians in the world of sport and to support churches as they build bridges into their communities through sport. Weir gives biblical justification for a positive view of sport, arguing that sport is a gift from God; part of God's creation; an opportunity for worship; an opportunity to love one's neighbour; a testing ground; and, an opportunity for witness. Sport should not be all-important and should not be the source of our significance as people.[3]

Sports Science research

Health, fitness, games and sport have now become the subjects of much research. The 1970's saw the first degrees in

Sports Studies and Sciences and the first edition of the Journal of Sports Science was published in 1983.

Research in these subject areas has helped us to understand more about how God made us. The benefits of regular exercise show that we are 'made to move'. The most recent research shows how important it is that learning and movement go together.

So, the obsession with sport that has led to some of the recent advances in exercise and movement science back up the case for an integration of physical activity with our Christian faith.

Summary

The church in the 21st century can be positive about movement activities, sport and games. God has made us to move and designed us to learn through movement. The next three chapters will help you to plan games and active learning sessions for children of all ages and will provide you with example activities, taken from the *Children's Ministry Teaching Programme*, one of the leading resources incorporating principles of active learning.

Certainly there is a problem with the idolization of sport and sports performers in our society, but, like Paul, we can use sport in order to communicate Christian truth. If we play sport ourselves, we can worship and witness as we do so.

Footnotes

1   Weir, Stuart. *What the Book says about Sport*. Bible Reading Fellowship, 2000. p. 20.

2   Peterson, Kurt W. *Muscular Christianity in Gale Encyclopedia of Popular Culture*, retrieved from www.findarticles.com

3   Weir, Stuart. *Towards a Theology of Sport* in *What the Book says about Sport*. Bible Reading Fellowship, 2000. pp.24-42.

4. Active Learning for Under 5s

The first five years of life are crucial to learning. Just think what a child can do by the age of five – he can walk, run, climb and dance, talk and sing, draw, paint, build and sculpt, interact with family, friends and strangers in keeping with his culture.

Development

Physical development
At birth a baby's brain comprises only about 25 per cent of its adult weight; at six months the brain will have reached 50 per cent of its adult weight and at five years 90 per cent. By five years, 90 per cent of base patterns may be formed, although they continue to be refined throughout life. Hence, the early years are fundamental to brain development.

The time from conception to 15 months after birth is critical for the vestibular system, situated in the inner ear and concerned with balance and the position of the body in space. Every movement stimulates the vestibular system and stimulates the brain for new learning. Our niece, Niamh, at one, has just learned to walk, a difficult feat of balance and co-ordination, showing that her vestibular system is developing well. Development of hearing, touch, smell, taste and sight follow in sequence after the vestibular sytem.

The neuromuscular system begins with reflex movements and then moves to the core muscles. A baby first begins to move from the core muscles. She first overcomes the flexor reflex of the foetal position and then learns to lift her head, developing strength in the neck and upper back. She learns to roll over, sit with and then without support, and finally crawl, stand, walk and run as she grows and develops and gains control of limb muscles.

Crawling, a cross-lateral movement, is important since both hemispheres and all lobes of her brain are activated together.

She begins to imitate the movements of older children and adults, which can appear quite comical at times. She imagines herself performing the action, which causes neural pathways in her brain to begin to form prior to her first imperfect attempts. Toddlers whose parents are worship leaders can often be seen 'singing with a microphone' or 'playing the guitar' in our church meetings as they watch Mum or Dad at the front.

Around four there is a major growth spurt in the areas of the brain concerned with vision, hearing, balance and other senses enabling children to progress quickly.

Social development

One year olds hardly notice each other. At 15 months interaction begins as the limbic system in the brain begins to develop. Around two children 'become' the emotion and outbursts are common. Between two and three they develop the concept of 'I' and begin to understand family relationships. Around three they begin to develop altruism and empathy.

Potential difficulties

Young children do not always receive the stimulation they need in order to develop their neuromuscular system in the normal way. Children who have not experienced sufficient movement opportunities appear clumsy and stiff. They cannot judge strength, speed or distance and seem to be more accident-prone. Some of the reasons children may have problems with physical tasks are given below.

Lack of attention

Children without sufficient attention and stimulation when very young, for example, orphans and neglected children, often grow up with developmental problems. Children more likely to thrive are those who have been cuddled, who have experienced a good deal of human interaction and who have been given a wide range of sensory experiences.

The act of being touched increases the production of Nerve Growth Factor (NGF), a hormone on the brain, which activates nerve net development. It also increases the synthesis of a neurotransmitter in the brain.[1] However, children do have the capacity to catch up. For example, a six-month-old baby had a developmental age of only two months when she arrived from an orphanage in Columbia. After three months with her adoptive parents in a stimulating environment she had caught up with her nine-month-old peers.[2] Similarly, Tia, a severely neglected child for the first two years of her life, made fantastic progress once placed in a loving family. Predictions that she may never walk or talk were proved wrong by the time she reached three.

Touch is necessary but we are of course all aware of the fear of inappropriate touch, although with the under five age group a comforting cuddle or a reassuring hand on the shoulder is still generally deemed acceptable.

Too much television

Young children with reduced movement and sensory experience for other reasons can have similar developmental problems. For example, television watching reduces first-hand experience of the environment and movement. Objects are seen two dimensionally instead of three dimensionally and natural eye movement is diminished. These factors both affect eye muscle and sight development. Children do not touch the objects seen and cannot tell whether events portrayed are 'real' or 'pretend'. Which are television tricks? What can really happen and what cannot?

Young children do not have the background experience to discriminate and understand in the way that older children and adults do. Posture and limb control are also negatively effected by lack of movement. Young children need to run, swing, roll, rock and spin in order to stimulate development of the vestibular system that controls balance and affects eye-limb co-ordination.

In the adult brain, the left brain processes one stimulus at a time while the right brain can process a cluster of stimuli all at once. While watching television, the left brain is hardly active at all. The right brain registers the television images but cross-referencing between left and right brain does not occur. Babies have unspecialized brains – it takes about twelve years for the left and right brain to fully specialize. Thought begins in a non-verbal way, for example, face recognition. As language develops, the brain begins to specialize. However, in infants watching many hours of television, the non-verbal 'right hemisphere' functions dominate for longer. There is a period during which the brain is ready for language development, but if there is a lack of conversation with the child and too much passive television watching, speech may not develop in the normal way. It can be hard to make up for this deficiency later.[3]

Television watching produces similar brain waves to those observed in sleep and in sensory deprivation experiments. Such experiments have been used in preparation for manned space flights.

Volunteers floated motionless in water at blood heat, in total silence. They wore goggles to exclude light and gloves to reduce their sense of touch. Many volunteers fell asleep but on waking some experienced hallucinations and dreams and distorted impressions of their bodies, such as the feeling that their arms or legs were growing or floating away. These experiments showed how normal sensory experience is vital to maintain a balanced state of mind.[4]

To remember something, it is best if senses, emotions and movement are all involved. Repetition, imagination and physical play all contribute to the process of learning.

Throughout life, hands-on experience increases learning efficiency. If touch is combined with the other senses more of the brain is activated.

Television watching, on the whole, is a passive process where the child misses out on the complex interplay between mental, emotional and physical involvement that is necessary for effective learning. We must not, however, forget programmes such as *Blue Peter* and *Art Attack* which promote a wide range of activities away from the television.

Lack of movement opportunities

Even the amount of time spent in a car seat could restrict children's development. In 1960, a child might have only spent 200 hours in the car in the first two years of its life. Even while in the car, children were not usually strapped in and so were crawling round and very active – not to be recommended of course, due to safety concerns! Nowadays, a child might spend 600 hours in the car in the first two years of its life. All of that time will be spent strapped into a car seat. So that's a reduction of 600 hours of motion development time.[5]

In addition, babies are often seated in this type of seat at home, while visiting other people's homes or attending church. Instead of lying them down which aids the development of their neck and back muscles, parents often strap them into a supportive seat to keep them safe and the baby cannot move freely.

Practical ideas

Along with the considerations outlined above, the results of a New York study of 133 individuals from infancy to adulthood should also influence our work with under 5's. This study showed that competency in adulthood was strongly linked with three factors in early life:

- Rich, sensory environments, outdoors and indoors
- Freedom to explore the environment with few restrictions
- Available parents (or other adults) to answer the child's questions.[6]

Remember that activities for under 5's need to be simple, mainly individual and non-competitive. Children of this age are not ready for team or group activities and will need close supervision. Leaders will often need to demonstrate what to do and perform any actions with the children, except in the case of more unstructured active play.

• Use rhymes with actions to gain attention

This sort of rhyme can be used and repeated regularly each time you want the children to look at you ready for the next instruction. The children will need to look at you to see which action they should be joining in with. By the end of the rhyme, most children should be sitting ready.

EXAMPLE: LOOK AT ME

Wiggle your fingers,
Pat your knees.
Fold your arms,
And look at me.

• Use rhymes with actions to make a teaching point

The following example teaches about prayer, reinforcing where, when and how to pray.

EXAMPLE: WHERE AND WHEN TO PRAY

Say the rhyme, with actions and expressions, and repeat for children to join in. You will need bells or tambourines.

In the bath,	*Rub body.*
Up a tree,	*Climbing actions.*
Anywhere, that's fine for me.	*Stretch hands out.*
I can pray noisily.	*Stamp and jingle bells loudly.*
I can pray joyfully.	*Jump up and down and jingle bells.*
I can pray quietly.	*Jingle bells quietly.*
When I'm happy.	*Make a happy face.*
When I'm sad.	*Make a sad face.*
When I'm good.	*Make a good face.*
When I'm bad.	*Make a cross face.*
Anytime, anywhere,	*Stretch out one hand, then the other.*
I can talk to God in prayer.	*Make talking movements with hands.*

• Use rhymes with actions reinforce the main points of a story

You can use an action rhyme to follow up the Bible story and reinforce the main points of the story.

EXAMPLE: THANKING JESUS

This action rhyme can be used with the story of Jesus healing ten lepers (Luke 17:11-19). Show the actions, then repeat for children to copy.

Jesus cared for ten sick men. *Hold up ten fingers*
He made each one of them
well again. *Jump up and shout, 'Yes!'*
Nine men ran to town
right away. *Move fingers as if running.*
But one came back,
and stopped to say, *Hold up one finger.*
Thank you, Jesus! *Raise hands.*
Thank you, Jesus!

Action rhymes repeated several times, especially those with tunes, help children to access their *automatic memory*. This type of memory is triggered by simple associations – the rhythm, tune and actions become associated with the words.[7]

• **Use actions as you tell stories**

The stories and actions can be very simple for the youngest children and a little more complicated for those approaching school age.

EXAMPLE: GOD HELPS US

This is a simplified version of the story of David and Goliath with actions (1 Samuel 17:12-50):
David was a little boy. *Hold your hand near the ground.*

Goliath was a big giant of a man. *Hold your hand above your head*. **Giant Goliath wanted to fight little David**. *Hold one hand high and the other low*. **David knew God would help him. David threw a stone and Goliath fell down**. *Pretend to throw*. **God helped little David fight a big giant**. *Hold one hand low and the other high*. **God did a big thing**.

- **Provide suitable toys for active play linked to the story theme**

As stated earlier, children can learn plenty from their own creative play. The following play activities are linked to the Bible stories specified.

EXAMPLE: GOD LOVES CHILDREN

Matthew 19:13-15

Have a wide range of dolls available for play in the home area. Encourage the children to pretend that they are grown ups showing love to their children (the dolls).

EXAMPLE: SOLOMON BUILDS THE TEMPLE

1 Kings 8

Ask children to build the very best building they can with children's building blocks.

- **Give the children experience of experimenting with a variety of materials and objects**

Children love to experiment, touch and hold things. The first example could be used prior to the Bible story. The second example would be more suitable as a follow up activity.

EXAMPLE: GOD HELPED MOSES AND THE ISRAELITES

Exodus 14:5–31.

You will need a large bowl of water, old newspapers, and paper towels. Put the bowl of water on the newspapers and gather the children around it.

Today we're going to do an experiment with water. I'm going to use my hands to push the water to the sides of the bowl, and the bottom will be dry. Put your hands in the water, palms together, and push them apart. **It's not working. Let me try again.** Repeat.

It still isn't working. Who can help me? Choose a volunteer to put their hands in the water with yours. **I think we need more help.** Repeat, gradually adding all the children. **Let's put all of our hands close together and have one last try.**

Try the experiment again. Children can dry their hands and sit down.

Why can't we push the water to the sides of the bowl? Children offer suggestions. **We can't do it, because it's impossible! Impossible means we can't do it.**

EXAMPLE: GOD CREATED THE WORLD.

These ideas could be used with the Genesis 1 story. If possible, take the children outside to explore nature at their own pace. Bring in natural items for the children to examine. For example:

Leaves to make rubbings

Fruit to touch and taste

Feathers to stick onto paper

Nuts and seeds to sort into their kinds

Flowers to press and make pictures
Water to pour and play with
Sand to dig and scoop and draw in

• **Give the children physical challenges and adapt well-known games**

Many games and challenges can be adapted to fit in with your teaching point or Bible story. Here is an example.

EXAMPLE: IMPOSSIBLE!

This is a starter activity to introduce the topic of impossibility. You could use it before any story where God does something that we would consider impossible. You will need two circles of coloured paper and reusable adhesive putty.

Fix the circles to the floor a short distance apart. Children can try jumping from one to the other. The circles can be moved further apart for greater challenge, until it becomes impossible.

• **When you ask the children questions, enable them to be active as they answer**

The following type of activity could be used to follow up almost any Bible story. It is a simple type of active quiz.

EXAMPLE: ACTIVE QUIZ

This quiz is based on Mark 8:22-26. Draw and colour four simple but different trees. Stick them around your meeting room. Stand everyone in the centre. Point out the trees.

Choose a tree and run to it. Why did the man's

friends bring him to Jesus? (*He needed help.*) **Choose another tree and run to it. What did Jesus do to help the blind man?** *(He touched his eyes and helped him see.)* **Choose another tree and run to it. Why was Jesus able to help the blind man see?** *Encourage children's response.* **Choose another tree and run to it. What does Jesus do when we need help?** *(Jesus cares and helps us.)*

- **Use objects and actions if you want to have some sort of discussion time**

This method is particularly useful for introducing a topic or for summing up at the end of a session. The following is a starter activity to introduce the theme of talking to God.

EXAMPLE: WE CAN TALK TO GOD

You will need a plastic cup; a storybook; a hairbrush; a shoe; a toothbrush; a toy or game; a cardboard box. In advance, cut a hold in the top of the box and put all the items inside. In turn, invite children to take an item from the box.

What is it? *Children respond.* **Who tells you, 'It's time for juice?/time to brush your teeth/hair, put your shoes on?' Who reads you stories? Who do you play with?**

People talk *make talking movements with hands* **to us about lots of different things from the time** *make clock hands* **we get up in the morning** *stand up, yawn and stretch,* **to the time** *make clock hands* **we go to sleep** *yawn and lay head on hands. Close eyes.* **We listen** *point to ears* **to people from the time** *make clock hands* **we get up in the morning** *stand up, yawn and stretch,* **to the time** *make clock hands* **we go to sleep** *yawn and lay head on hands. Close eyes.*

• Make prayers active

Children under five may not pray very long prayers but they can pray simply. They do not have to say words to pray. Making prayers active can be a useful way of helping them to participate even if they don't speak. Here are some ideas to get you started:

1   Seat the children in a circle and pass something round linked to your story or theme e.g. toy lamb, a heart shape, a small mirror or shiny spoon. Pray as they pass it round.
2   Children can put on a hat or spectacles when it is their turn to pray or be prayed for.
3   Children can move into a special seat, stand up, run to the middle, or move around the room as they pray or while someone prays for them.
4   Ask the children to clap in rhythm while you pray.
5   Ask children to express their prayers using a musical instrument.

Footnotes

1   Hannaford, Carla. *Smart Moves: Why learning is not all in your head.* Great Ocean Publishers, Arlington, Virginia, USA, 1995. p39.
2   Cheatum, Billye Ann, and Hammond, Allison A. *Physical Activities for Improving Children's Learning and Behaviour: A Guide to Sensory Motor Development.* Human Kinetics, USA, 2000. p39.
3   Clouder, Christopher, Jenkinson, Sally, and Large, Martin. (ed.) *Out of the Box* in *The Future of Childhood.* Hawthorne Press, UK, 2000. pp91-110.
4   ibid.
5   *An Interview with Eric Jensen,* Brain based learning expert. Retrieved from www.cascd.org
6   Hannaford, Carla. *Smart Moves: Why learning is not all in your head.* Great Ocean Publishers, Arlington, Virginia, USA, 1995. p48.
7   Sprenger, Marilee. *Learning and Memory – The Brain in Action.* www.ascd.org/readingroom/books/sprenger99book.html.

5. Active Learning for 5-9s

Between five and nine children change dramatically in the way they relate to other people, becoming far less dependent upon their parents and other adults and forming important friendships. They grow physically taller and the development of both their brain and body allows them to perform more complex gross and fine motor skills.

Development

Physical development
Between the ages of five and nine children's motor skills improve dramatically, enabling them to enjoy more complicated games and challenges. Most children will learn to ride a bike, swim and skate/blade during this period. Most will learn to hit a ball with a bat and write fluently. They will be keen to master new skills, some children exhibiting more perseverance than others. These new abilities are linked to a major growth spurt in the frontal lobes of the brain at

around age eight. The frontal lobes of the motor cortex contain areas that control specific muscles all over the body and which are concerned with learning skilled movements. The main part of the brain, the cerebrum, is divided into two hemispheres. The left hemisphere usually deals with logic functions – numbers, patterns, parts, details, structures, plans and technique. The right hemisphere usually deals with 'the whole' – image, intuition, flow, emotion, feelings, creativity. At birth, both hemispheres contain all functions but specialization occurs during childhood.

Typically, the right hemisphere of the brain develops and enlarges between the ages of four and seven. The left brain enlarges between ages seven and nine. Taking this into account, perhaps activities involving reading, spelling and numbers (logical, sequential activities) should not be a major concern at four or five, as usually happens in the UK. Consider making active and creative activities involving plenty of dialogue and the expression of emotion the major part of children's education up to age seven.

Social development

One of the key changes as children start school is that they learn how to make friends and co-operate. They will also be very determined that everything is 'fair'. This means that team and co-operative activities become possible which open up a wider range of movement activities.

We should remember that unstructured play helps children learn co-operation, creativity, altruism and understanding. Children's leisure time becomes more organized during this period as they become involved in after school and weekend clubs. Their lives can be tightly scheduled by their parents and they are often told to 'hurry up'. They need time to experience life at their own pace. High-speed activity in computer games, TV and video and lack of natural rhythm through experience of nature gives children a distorted idea of time.

Imaginative and creative play is important – it is not necessary or beneficial for children to be constantly entertained and organized. When we were at primary school our favourite place to go was 'down in the dip'. This was a wild area that sloped downwards. It was fun to explore and make up games there. At one point a tree house, some huge pipes and other shelters were added. The best fun was to use loose planks to make our own dens. We certainly learned about co-operation, leadership and creativity.

Potential difficulties

Understanding the problems children of this age may face will help us to be sympathetic to children we care for when they are not able or willing to join in with an activity we have planned.

Emotions and learning

The frontal lobes of the motor cortex are connected with the limbic system, part of the brain involved in emotional processing. Emotions are expressed through the body. Emotions interpret the experience and determine our response. For example, depending upon whether it is positive and useful or stressful and scary, different neurotransmitters are released. If the event is perceived as a positive learning experience, neurotransmitters which increase our ability to form or reorganize neural networks are released.[1] However, if the event is stressful, adrenaline prepares the body for a fight/flight response. With adrenaline comes cortisol that decreases our ability to learn and remember.

This emotion-movement-learning connection can therefore be positive or negative. On the one hand, activities that are fun, exciting or dramatic aid learning. On the other, if learning activities are perceived as too stressful, perhaps due to a mis-match of teaching and learning style or the presentation of subject material which is far too difficult, learning is inhibited.

Bodily-kinesthetic learners and stress
Unfortunately for bodily-kinesthetic learners, as they enter school their learning tends to become less active. As they get older, they increasingly have to learn to sit still on the floor while their teacher reads them a story and shows them words and numbers and pictures. They increasingly have to sit still in their chairs while they carry out reading, writing and maths activities.

Tests increasingly involve still, quiet conditions. Most education relies too heavily on language, failing to involve the senses, emotions and the learner's whole body as teachers work hard to prepare children for Key Stage 1, and later, Key Stages 2 and 3, national tests.

If children become stressed their learning will be inhibited. Frequent teaching in a style contrary to a child's learning style may result in failure and stress so they become even less likely to learn. This is what happens with many bodily-kinesthetic learners. In addition, their liking for movement and fidgeting will probably get them into trouble at school and that will cause additional stress. Often the punishment of missed break times will exacerbate the problem as, on many school days break times will be the only time children have the freedom to move!

Apart from a general increase in learning through movement in the classroom, there are two methods I have heard of to try to address this problem. One teacher, at times when children must sit and listen, placed the fidgeting children at the back with a small piece of play dough or similar to handle while she spoke. Another teacher, rather than using a missed break time as a punishment, gave out laps of the playground – rather controversial though, as we do not want children to associate physical activity with punishment. Perhaps extra movement breaks as a reward would be more positive.

You will almost certainly encounter these lively children in your group and will have to work hard to make the learning experience positive for them. The more they can move, the better! Interestingly, Sunday morning children's sessions at our church are very active times and many of the leaders would not realize that several children in their group are having difficulties at school either academically or behaviourally.

Children under stress will tend to display either a fight or flight response. Typical 'fight' responses will be actions such as hitting other children, throwing books or other items, speaking or shouting rudely and aggressively, and destroying work or equipment. Typical 'flight' responses tend to be frequent requests to go to the toilet, saying they are tired or bored, daydreaming, and forgetting to bring things that they need. One child I taught used to get his fingers stuck in the window catch or hide under some cushions as 'flight' responses.

While bodily-kinesthetic learners may display symptoms of stress if asked to keep still and quiet, other learners may display these symptoms if asked to become involved in active games! Competition in the form of races, ball games and team games are unlikely to suit all the children in your group so watch out for signs of stress in other children while catering for the needs of the energetic ones. There's no need to force everyone to take part in everything all of the time.

Children with specific difficulties

If not identified previously, as they start school any children with special needs should begin to be given help in the necessary areas and their needs may become more obvious in your group. For some of these children activities involving movement will be excellent, e.g. children with ADD (Attention Deficit Disorder)/ADHD (Attention Deficit and Hyperactivity Disorder) and those who find reading and writing difficult, although they may require extra help to carry out tasks as suggested. For others, movement activities will be good for them but the children may find them difficult – they may have poor muscle tone, be clumsy, or as with children with autism, dislike interaction. It is important for them not to feel embarrassed. You need to create a supportive atmosphere where everybody's efforts are valued and no one is ridiculed.

For others, e.g. those with impaired sight or loss of use of one or more limbs, it may seem at first glance that an activity will be impossible for them. However, it may be that with a supportive partner or help from a leader they can still join in successfully.

If a child, for whatever reason, cannot or does not want to join in, try to involve them by asking them to help keep score, or be a 'team captain' or 'manager'.

To gain further understanding in the area of physical and behavioural difficulties in children and ideas of how to help them read *Physical Activities for Improving Children's Learning and Behaviour – A Guide to Sensory Motor Development* by Billye Ann Cheatum and Allison A. Hammond.

Practical ideas

Children of this age are normally full of life and enthusiasm and you should have no trouble in getting them to take part in action-packed sessions.

• Use actions as you are telling stories

Making a craft or passing round props are good ways to help children remain active in a constructive way while you are telling them a story. You can also involve them in actions. Children can perform a certain action every time a key word is mentioned, or they can follow a leader's example in miming some of the feelings and events in the story. This example shows how actions can be used in the story of the Prodigal Son.

EXAMPLE: THE IMPATIENT YOUNG MAN

This is a simplified version of Luke 15:11–24.
The children, in pairs, can all do actions while someone reads the story aloud.

This is a story Jesus told to show how much our heavenly Father loves us, and that we can be forgiven for the wrong things we do. The young man in Jesus' story was very impatient with his father. He couldn't wait to get his hands on his father's money.

Action: Show what an impatient son would look like.

Action: Loving father tries to put his arm around his son, who turns away.

The young man said to his father, 'Dad, I want my share of your money now. I can't wait any longer.'

Action: Son shakes his father's arm.

The father was sad, but gave his son part of the family money.

Action: Father gives money to his son, who puts it in his pocket.

The son took the money and went far away from home.

Action: Son walks away from his father without turning round to wave goodbye.

He spent all his money on parties.

Action: Son dances.

Soon, he had a problem.

Action: Son turns his pockets inside out.

'Oh, no!' he cried. 'There's no money left! Not even enough for food or somewhere to stay!'

All the new friends he had made suddenly didn't want to be his friend anymore.

Continue in a similar way.

Use the actions to help you to engage the feelings of the children. *Emotional memory strategies* are the most powerful of all so it is important that the children can take part in the sense of sadness, celebration, anger, etc. felt by the story characters.

By dressing up to tell the story, providing a few props or pieces of scenery, telling the Bible story from a different area of the room each week, or even telling the story out of doors, you will help to stimulate the children's *episodic memory*. This type of memory is triggered by location – the visual memory of the location will assist children's memory of the content of what was taught there.[2]

This is partly why holiday club and Kidz Klub style storytelling is so memorable and effective. Our recent *TreasureZone* holiday sessions featured a jungle backdrop and characters with whom the children could identify as they found out about Jesus and searched for the Treasure of God's Kingdom.[3] The children's emotional memory and episodic memory pathways were stimulated so that even in the front-led parts of the programme the children were well involved.

- ## Use actions and movement activities to learn memory verses

Some verses of the Bible are ideal for making up actions. You can also use movement in other ways, for example:

1 Write out the words on separate pieces of card. Give one word to each child and ask them to rearrange themselves into the correct order. To make it more interesting, write the words on suitable props or pictures depending on the story you have been reading that session, e.g. 'flames', stones, 'sheep'.

2 Cut wool into short strands. 'Write' out the memory verse on the floor or on a blanket using the wool. Read

the memory verse several times with the children and then ask them to remove a few strands at a time. Repeat the verse together until there is nothing left on the blanket.

3 Write the words of the memory verse on stepping stones or a hopscotch grid. Children can say the words as they step, hop or jump across them.

Using actions to learn memory verses is another example of an *automatic memory strategy*, where material is remembered through association. If asked to learn a memory verse, I have found that many children in our church will choose to make up actions as they find this the most effective memory strategy for this type of task.

• Use rhymes with actions to reinforce key points of stories or the main message of the session

Either show the children actions for them to join in with as a leader reads out the rhyme or read or sing the rhyme and ask children to make up their own actions.

EXAMPLE: FIRE ON THE MOUNTAIN

This rhyme is based on 1 Kings 18:16–46 and reinforces the main points of the story.

Mark a dividing line with masking tape. Choose someone lively to be Elijah. Stand Elijah on one side and everyone else on the other side of the line. Chant each stanza for children to repeat loudly with you.

Elijah: **I'm on God's side. I'm on God's side.**
I'm on God's side, and here I'll stay.
Others, jumping backwards and forwards over the line:
We can't decide. We can't decide.
We can't decide. What shall we do?
Others, kneeling and praying:
Baal, show your power. Baal show your power.
Baal, show your power. Show us now!
Others, jumping up and down:
Baal doesn't answer. Baal doesn't answer.
Baal doesn't answer. Where's his power?
Elijah: **I'll show you God's power. I'll show you God's**
power. I'll show you God's power. Show you now!
Others, shielding their faces:
We see God's power. We see God's power.
We see God's power. Wow! Wow! Wow!
Others, crossing the line, kneel by Elijah:
We're on God's side. We're on God's side.
We're on God's side, and here we'll stay!

• Make quizzes active

If you are going to have a quiz, perhaps as a follow up to
the Bible story, make it active by using a method such as one
of those below:

EXAMPLE: RUN TO THE ANSWER

Give children multiple choice answers, A, B or C and have
them run to a different wall depending on which answer
they think is correct.

For example, **Why did God tell Noah to build the ark?**

a   To save the animals

b   Because Noah found favour with God (correct answer)

c   To see if it could be done

EXAMPLE: ACT THE ANSWER

Give children multiple choice answers and have them perform a different action depending on which answer they think is correct. For example:

Who did Simon Peter meet?

a   A man lying begging who could not walk *(lie down)* (correct answer)

b   A man hobbling with a bad leg *(stand on one leg)*

c   A man busking to get money *(pretend to play a violin)*

The answers to these questions are not supposed to be difficult. I find that most children have no trouble in running to the right part of the room or acting out the correct answer. The story is reviewed without confusion and the children feel they have succeeded. If the method for gaining points explained in the next example is used in combination with one of the above methods, the quiz will be more exciting.

EXAMPLE: EARNING POINTS

When a child provides the correct answer to a question think of an interesting, active way of giving them points. They could run and pick a pebble for their team. The pebble will have a number written on the bottom that tells them how many points they have earned. Alternatively they could aim a ball or beanbag at a bucket or target, roll a ball at skittles or kick a football at a goal to earn points.

Some of our children who appear to have no interest in a quiz where they just sit and put up their hands to answer become excited participants when a running, throwing or kicking task is involved.

- **Use physical challenges and games to re-inforce a teaching point or as a story reminder**

Many common games can be adapted for use in your teaching sessions. Here are a couple of games and challenges that could be used to either introduce or back up a teaching point.

EXAMPLE: ISLANDS

This activity could be used to introduce or back up a passage such as Mark 10:13-16 where Jesus welcomes children. Make newspaper islands on the floor. Have children move around your playing space. Call out a number and instruct children to make groups of exactly that number on the newspaper islands. Any children left out can help referee as the game continues. Remove an island for each round. Finish the game by calling out the total number of children to try to stand on one remaining island.

Afterwards, ask the children how they felt when they were left out – lonely? Not wanted? Shut out? Tell them that sometimes people we think are our friends treat us like that and leave us out. Jesus will never leave us out. He has the power to always be our friend.

Watch out for smaller children during this game – the

larger, rougher children are liable to have an unfair advantage. When smaller children reach an island first, make sure they don't get pushed off, as started to happen when we played this recently.

• Make prayers active

Most children of this age quickly learn to pray out loud. Here are some ideas to make prayer active:

1 Children can throw paper aeroplanes to each other with prayers written on them. Children pray the prayer on the aeroplane they receive.
2 Throw a ball or beanbag round a circle of children. Children pray a short sentence when they receive the ball/bean bag.
3 Use a 'Pass the parcel'-type activity with prayers included in each wrapping. A Treasure Hunt activity could work in a similar way.
4 Use a parachute, flags, or ribbons as you pray. These may be particularly suitable for prayers of praise.

Footnotes

1 Hannaford, Carla. *Smart Moves: Why learning is not all in your head.* Great Ocean Publishers, Arlington, Virginia, USA, 1995. p53.
2 Sprenger, Marilee. *Learning and Memory – The Brain in Action.* www.ascd.org/readingroom/books/sprenger99book.html.
3 *The TreasureZone Holiday Club – The Children's Ministry Teaching Programme.* Children's Ministry, Kingsway Communications Ltd., UK, 2003.

6. Active Learning for Over 9s

At some point children over nine begin to experience the onset of puberty. They begin the roller-coaster ride of the process of becoming an adult. 'Tweenager' is becoming a word used to describe the phase where children, before they hit the teenage years, start turning into mini young adults. From a younger and younger age their clothes and purchasing choices seem to be those of children trying to become adults rather too soon.

Development

Physical development
Children's physiological stage of development between nine and eleven normally shows that they are still children, although some, especially girls do begin puberty as young as eight or nine. Most obviously, puberty brings a fast spurt of height increase and development of sex organs. Girls, on average, grow very quickly between twelve and thirteen,

reaching adult height by eighteen. Boys normally grow fastest between fourteen and fifteen, finishing growing at around twenty. Hands and feet grow first, followed by shin and forearm bones, then thigh and upper arms, then the spine. Lastly, the chest broadens in boys and the hips and pelvis widen in girls.

Between nine and twelve the Corpus Callosum that connects the two hemispheres of the brain develops further and allows for more efficient whole brain processing. Learning experiences that integrate as many brain areas as possible will assist this process.

Social development
Peers begin to become more important than parents and rapid changes of mood are often evident as the teenage years approach. Some children of this age can be very shy, others can be very unco-operative. Children want to become more independent and think many of their parent's views are completely ridiculous.

Potential difficulties
Any difficulties in using games and movement with this age group are likely to stem from the fast growth exhibited by some and the beginnings of teenage rebellion. The learning style of each child and any individual special needs will of course have an impact in the same way as for five to nine year olds.

Lack of co-ordination
Often, children's bodies grow so quickly that their brain cannot keep up. Their centre of gravity rises and muscle

and tendon receptors take time to develop. This leads to the clumsiness seen in many teenagers and should be taken into account when undertaking physical activities. Teenagers may be embarrassed at their lack of co-ordination and girls in particular may be embarrassed about their developing body.

Growth in both boys and girls is triggered by testosterone. Levels of this hormone are far higher in boys than in girls and this is why boys develop more muscle and generally become bigger and stronger than girls.

As children grow and develop it will often become more advantageous to separate boys and girls for some physical activity, whereas before puberty children would play together.

Discipline

Discipline can become more of an issue when dealing with this age group. Their moods and emotions, their desire to become independent, and their need to fit in with peers can all lead to problems for you as a leader. See the Appendix for help in this area.

Negative attitudes towards physical activity

Some children will have had a very negative experience of physical education at school. If they are not particularly athletic, often get picked last for teams and have been made fun of by others, they may be very unenthusiastic about joining in with active games. Avoid 'team captains' picking teams if certain children are always chosen last.

Try to ensure the less athletic group members can achieve success.

Practical activities

By nine, children will be more advanced in their motor skill development so will be more proficient in movement activities. They will enjoy faster and more complicated games. They will begin to understand abstract concepts so physical activities which illustrate concepts can be used, e.g. perseverance, obstacles, temptation. They will be able to handle simulation games. You may like to take your group away for a weekend and give them the chance to try outdoor and adventurous activities where they can learn valuable lessons about teamwork, trust and leadership, and cement or make new friendships with each other and with leaders.

• Use movement to help illustrate a Bible story

Older children may have gone beyond the stage of wanting to join in with simple actions, although when they are part of a group containing younger children they may join in quite happily. You will probably make more use of drama with this age group.

However, you can also use simpler movement activities. This may be particularly appropriate if the passage contains some difficult names of people and places.

EXAMPLE: AHAB AND ELIJAH

On the floor of your room, roughly mark out four areas representing (working from south to north) Judah, Israel, Samaria and Sidon. Give the following signs to six people: 'Asa, King of Judah'; 'Ahab, son of Omri'; 'Jereboam, son of Nebat'; 'Jezebel'; 'Ethball, king of Sidon'; 'Elijah of Tishbe in Gilead'. Explaining where you are placing them, stand Asa in Judah, Ahab astride Israel and Samaria, Jereboam in Israel (he should lie down as he is dead!), Jezebel with Ethball in Sidon and Elijah in Israel. As their names occur in the passage, they raise their placards in the air. Jezebel should move to Ahab's side when he marries her. Elijah should move to stand facing Ahab at the end of the passage. (If you have a small room and a small group, you may prefer to ask people to place named stickers on a map as you read.)

Ask a leader to read 1 Kings 16:29-33 and 17:1. The six people used as visual aids should make this passage full of names a little clearer. You can then ask some follow up questions.

• Make Bible story follow up active

You could also use the active quiz ideas in the five to nines section with this age group, making sure the questions are age appropriate. Below is another idea where the idea of an active quiz has been specially designed to suit the passage.

EXAMPLE: OVER THE CLIFF

Have a leader read Luke 8:26-39. Then, have everyone look at a copy of the passage in their Bibles before forming two teams, each with a spokesperson, to answer questions such as those overleaf in turn.

To make the quiz active, position the teams on a line in the middle of the room. Place three cones or markers behind them, evenly spaced, and three in front. A correct answer enables a team to move forward one marker. If they answer incorrectly, they must move back one marker. If they end up past back marker number three, they have 'fallen over the cliff' and are 'out'. Once on front marker three, a team remains there unless they answer incorrectly. Questions answered incorrectly can be passed to the other team. Who can survive until the end?

1 Mention four things that were strange about the man. *(He did not wear clothes; he did not live in a house; he lived in the tombs; he was very strong.)*
2 What did the man say that indicated that he was demon-possessed, rather than just mentally ill? *(He identified Jesus as the Son of God.)*
3 Why did he say his name was 'Legion'? *(Many demons had gone into him.)*
4 How do we know that this region, across the lake from Galilee, was probably inhabited mainly by Gentiles (non-Jews)? *(A herd of pigs was there. Jews did not keep pigs because they were 'unclean'.)*
5 Where did Jesus send the demons? *(Into the pigs.)*

Continue the questions in a similar way.

• Use physical challenges and games to back-up the theme or concept for the session

EXAMPLE: LOST AND FOUND

These 'treasure hunt'-style activities can be used with Luke 15.

1 Coin: Hide a £1 coin in the room before the session. As people arrive, challenge them to find it. If they do, the finder can hide it again for others to seek.

2 Sheep: Prior to the session, cut 100 pieces of wool of approximately equal length (about 10cm) and tie them loosely to articles all around the room. If possible use other rooms too.

99 of the pieces of wool should be fairly easy to find, but tie one piece in a completely hidden and very unlikely place. Challenge your group to collect all 100 pieces of wool – you may need to give some clues to help them to find the last one.

If the weather is fine and you a have safe area that would be suitable, do this activity outside. If you have a large group, plenty of space and someone to help you tie the wool pieces, cut 200 pieces: 100 of one colour and 100 of another colour. You can then split the group into two teams for the search. Only give a prize if all 100 wool pieces are found.

EXAMPLE: BIG SPENDER

This is an example of a 'life size' board game. It could be used to introduce the story of the Prodigal Son. Using sheets of A4 paper or card numbered 1-30, lay out a pathway around your room. On certain numbers, add instructions such as the following:

Spend £200 on new clothes	Spend £100 on CDs
Lose £100 on arcade games	Spend £50 on trainers
Spend £100 on video games	Pay a £500 hotel bill
Spend £400 on a new bike	Spend £250 on train fares
Pay a £150 mobile phone bill	Spend £150 at a restaurant

Move forward two steps

Make sure that instructions occur every two or three steps

so that there is a high likelihood of players landing on 'spend' numbers. On numbers 28, 29 and 30 write 'Blow any money left on a party and move on to the finish'. It will be fairly difficult for players to reach the end without loosing all their money.

To start the game, give each player '£1000' in '£50 notes' (use toy money or make your own) and let them take turns to roll a die. As in a normal board game players move forward according to the number on the die and follow any instruction written on the number on which they land. Money 'spent' should be handed to a leader. Any player spending all their money before they reach the end can use up one go taking out a 'loan' from the 'bank' (the leader with the money).

The first person to reach the end, having spent all their money, is the 'winner'. The prize however should be something revolting and undesirable – e.g. an ice cream tub full of 'pig swill' made from left over food and vegetable peelings mixed with water.

You could give every player a prize when they finish – those with no money receive 'pig swill' while those with money left can exchange each '£50 note' for a biscuit or sweet.

Explain that this activity gave examples of some of the ways a young person nowadays might choose to spend their money.

Spending it in those ways might be rather selfish but if at the end of the day they live with one or both parents who provide for all their basic needs it wouldn't matter too much if they blew all the money on extravagant things. Move on to introduce the Bible story.

- ## Use physical challenges and games to act as story reminders

EXAMPLE: SHEPHERD AND THIEVES

This game could be used to introduce John 10:4-5.

You will need one person to play the part of the 'shepherd', two people to play the part of 'thieves', and three or more people to play the part of 'sheep'. All the sheep should be blindfolded and asked to stand in the middle of the room. The 'shepherd' and the 'thieves' should stand around the edge.

The shepherd's task is to lead the sheep around the room following a simple obstacle course shown to him by a leader. He/she may address the sheep collectively, i.e. 'sheep', or he/she may use individual names when necessary to redirect any that stray off course. If the sheep successfully reach the end of the course they have reached 'safe pastures' (i.e. give them some biscuits as a prize.)

The thieves' role is to shout confusing directions to try to make sheep bump into the side walls or stray outside lines marking the playing area. Any that do are successfully 'stolen' (i.e. they're out of the game). If you require more space, find a safe area outside, weather permitting.

EXAMPLE: STORY RELAY

Relays can be used in many situations. This one is a 'temple-building relay' based on the Jews' journey back to Jerusalem and the building of the temple (Ezra 1:5-11; 3:1-2; 3:7-10; 6:13-16). Play this relay game in two or more teams. Here are the instructions for each team:

1 When everyone is ready to start, they must wait seventy seconds before the word 'Go', representing the seventy years the Jews spent in Babylon.

2 A number of items representing articles of silver and gold, goods, livestock and gifts (foil trays, cuddly toys, boxes, etc. will do) must be taken to 'Jerusalem' (i.e. the other end of the room), in relay style.

3 Everyone must run to 'Jerusalem' together and build the 'altar' (use boxes or wooden blocks).

4 A 'cymbal' should be crashed five times to represent the completion of the temple foundations (you could use saucepan lids).

5 A sheet of paper must be taken to a leader for them to sign, representing the time of trouble and the decree needed from King Darius.

6 The 'temple' should be built using boxes and a loud shout given when it is finished, e.g. 'The temple is finished. Praise the Lord!'

Leaders will need to demonstrate first. Teams may need help in remembering what comes next as they progress. I find relays are among our most popular activities.

• When you want to discuss choices and opinions, use a movement activity

The following type of activity could also be used with younger age groups.

EXAMPLE: TEMPTOMETER

This could be used as a starter activity for Luke 4, where Jesus is tempted in the desert. Mark a large, basic thermometer on the floor using masking tape and paper numbers. This will be your 'temptometer'. Have everyone stand beside the temptometer and then call out temptations such as those below. Each person must run to an appropriate 'temperature' on the temptometer (high numbers = very tempted, low number = not so tempted).

1 Copying someone else's answers during a test.
2 Moving one of your friend's pawns in a chess game while they are answering the phone.
3 Taking a £1 coin that you find on the classroom floor.
4 Watching an '18' video at a friend's house.
5 Losing your temper when asked to tidy your room yet again.

Add more of you own. Afterwards, discuss which temptations are the hardest to resist and why.

• Use simulation games to help older children to understand someone else's situation

The following example can used to introduce older children to the topic of wealth and poverty.

EXAMPLE: GOTTALOTS AND HAVENOTS

This could be part of a session about worshipping as God desires, based on Isaiah 1:1-4; 11-20.

At the end of the last session, you should have asked your group to miss breakfast (or whatever meal would come just before your session) today. Make sure they know they should have a drink, but not eat. At the start of the session, find out who has remembered not to eat and assign them to the 'Havenots' group. Anyone who has eaten by mistake, or who did not realize the instruction had been given, should be assigned to the 'Gottalots' group. If everyone has remembered not to eat, randomly pick a few individuals to be 'Gottalots'. Gottalots should be seated on chairs at one end of the room whilst 'Havenots' should be seated on the floor at the other end.

Announce that you will now provide breakfast (or lunch/tea) for everyone. Ask them not to start eating immediately. Provide a good meal for the 'Gottalots' (cereals, rolls, croissants, bacon... whatever you can manage) but provide the 'Havenots' (the majority of the group) with just a loaf of bread and jug of water to share between them.

Prior to beginning the meal, explain these rules. 'Gottalots' may eat whatever they like but, when they hear a leader ring a bell or blow a whistle they must go to a separate table with a small portion of food (a 'sacrifice') and bow before returning to their breakfast. 'Havenots' may only eat the bread and water given to them, but, a few at a time, they may visit the 'Gottalots' and try to obtain extra food by begging or offering to do a task (e.g. pouring the drinks out, serving food, promising to clear up afterwards). The 'Gottalots' can decide whether to share their food.

Afterwards, discuss the feelings of the 'Havenots' and 'Gottalots'. Explain that in Israel at the time you will be reading about today there were many things wrong. One problem was the bad treatment of the poor by the rich. Later in the session you can apply what you learn to our world today.

This experience should certainly be lodged firmly in the childrens' minds via their emotional memory pathway.

When I ran a similar activity with a group of ten-year-olds, the 'Havenots' could not believe that they really weren't going to get a fair deal. It certainly made them think!

• Make prayer active

Several of the ideas for five to nines can also work well with the older age group. In addition, you may like to try:

1 Signing – Ask someone who knows sign language to teach you to pray using signs.
2 Prayer stations – Set up prayer stations around your room, or even the whole building. Stick up prayer requests and/or assign, label and decorate certain areas for specific types of prayer (e.g. saying 'thank you', saying 'sorry', praising God, praying for friends, praying for people abroad, praying about things in the news, praying for your local area). Children can walk around either alone or in pairs, praying silently or aloud. This can be particularly helpful for times when you want to have an extended period of prayer.
3 Prayer walks – Take the group around your local area and stop to pray in key places, e.g. schools, police stations, parks, shops, their own streets.

We have found that setting up a prayer room with prayer stations has proved particularly successful with all ages. I have seen 24-hour prayer set up for several weeks in two churches with pairs and groups taking an hour at a time to pray. Children and young people were involved in both cases.

7. Sport, Games and Evangelism

Sport, like music, is a huge part of our culture. In fact, those who play and watch sport could be described as the largest people group in the world.

As we discussed earlier, sport has become so important to many people that it has effectively become their god. However, as we have seen, sport and games are good in that they enable people to enjoy the physical activity that is so necessary for a healthy life. God has designed us to move and since physical activity has decreased to almost nil in many people's normal everyday lives, participation in sport and games can compensate.

Many people, including children, enjoy sport, and as Christians we can see the value of physical activity. Therefore, sport and games can be very effectively used in service and outreach to our communities.

Here are a variety of ways that you and your church may be able to serve your local community by providing sport and physical activity for children and families. As you will see, there are various ways that some biblical truth can also be incorporated.

My main involvement in children's sport at present is heading up Sportz Klub, an initiative of Kings Church, Eastbourne.

Sportz Klub

This runs lively, energetic Christian clubs for children in local schools. Our first clubs have started as after school clubs and have an indoor athletics focus with running, jumping and throwing skills and challenges. We plan to start further after school clubs in the future and hope to start clubs on Saturday mornings and during school holidays. Clubs consist of coaching, fun and competition and, where possible, children can work towards awards (e.g. shine:awards in athletics; football Star Challenge awards).

In addition to developing sports skills and fitness, each Sportz Klub session incorporates a theme from the Bible such as perseverance or teamwork – Christian values important both in sport and life in general.

Our first clubs, one for Years 3 and 4 and one for Years 5 and 6 have operated as ten week courses. The children have been very enthusiastic and by mid-way through several children had also started coming to our Saturday morning Kidz Klub, bringing other friends with them.

Programme for a Sportz Klub Session
Each 60-90 min session consists of:
1 First Half
   Welcome and warm-up
   Skill and fitness based challenges, games and activities

2 Half Time Team Talk
to include Sport Link, Bible Link and Life Link; sports
video clip
3 Second Half
Games, competitions, races and assessment for awards
Cool down and review

Example Sportz Klub Session Plans
Each session has a sports focus and a linked Bible focus:

- Session One: *Jumping.*
  The way to play: Rule books and coaching manuals help
  us to know the best way to play sport; the Bible tells us
  the best way to live life; following rules and advice is
  good (Deuteronomy 10:12-13).
- Session Two: *Balance and Agility.*
  Training: Sports people train hard to improve; being a
  Christian is like being in training; if you want to improve
  at something, you need to keep practicing (1 Timothy
  4:8).
- Session Three: *Hurdles.*
  Overcoming difficulties: Some athletes have obstacles to
  negotiate as they race, all athletes have difficulties to
  overcome; everyone, including Christians has difficulties
  to face in life; don't give up when something is difficult
  (Romans 12:21).
- Session Four: *Relays.*
  Teamwork: Relay runners and other sports people work
  together in a team, all with a special job to do; people
  who follow Jesus are like a team, working together
  with special abilities and jobs; be a good team member
  (1 Corinthians 12).

- Session Five: *Running (distance)*.
  Perseverance: Distance runners and other sports people need lots of perseverance; Christians need to persevere in following Jesus, it's not always easy; keep trying to do your best even when things are hard and you feel fed up (Hebrews 12:1).
- Session Six: *Throwing*.
  Setting aims and goals: all athletes have goals for which they are aiming; Christians have the goal of being like Jesus; what are your aims in life? (Hebrews 12:2)

Volunteers must be church members over 16, have a keen interest in sport and possess the ability to work with children. All volunteers must undergo a Criminal Records Bureau (CRB) check. Basic training in sports coaching is provided and volunteers are encouraged to gain relevant coaching qualifications.

Tumbling toddlers

I have noticed that the soft play sessions for toddlers at the local leisure centre are hugely popular. Big, soft blocks, rockers and mats are provided for children to climb, jump, rock and roll on. Given the importance of the development of the vestibular system described earlier, this is physiologically excellent and great fun for the kids.

Could this sort of equipment be provided in your church? It would be an excellent addition to any normal parent and toddler club already in existence or it could form a new way of attracting families. In my experience, a parent and toddler group works most effectively as an outreach tool if some very simple Bible input is included, perhaps using a puppet (see *Children's Ministry Teaching Programme –*

Under 3's Leader's Guide). A 'Just Looking' or 'Alpha' group can be organised alongside for the parents.

Monthly sports fun

If you are rather short of facilities, and/or time, why not consider running a monthly sports fun group for children? Our church runs a Year 6 Club on Friday evenings once a month. Although not entirely sport/physical activity based, some of the children's favourite activities are swimming, Laser Quest, football and other games. It is really just a social activity but is very easy for children to bring their friends to so it is a bridge-builder with families outside the church.

Sports teams

Some churches actually run children's sports teams, particularly football. If you're considering this, think carefully about the following:

- Will the team only include church children or will others be included?
- Will there be any spiritual input or direct link with church activities?
- If not, will the time commitment and effort involved lead to great football results but no or little evangelistic results?

It may be more appropriate for children to be part of local clubs where they and their families can make friends outside the church and build bridges. However, if Sunday training and matches are a problem, a church team can provide alternative opportunities. If you, or other children and parents, are struggling over the issue of Sunday sport, I would recommend the chapter on Sunday sport in Stuart Weir's book *What the Book says about Sport*. Do remember that sporty children need loads of active fun and encouragement in their church groups, otherwise sports teams soon become more exciting and important to them and they may become infrequent visitors to your group.

One-off events

Use your church building or church hall or hire a suitable hall and hold one-off sports and games mornings, evenings, Saturdays, Holiday Clubs, etc! Below are some ideas:

- Invite a local Christian sports person who could come as a special guest to coach, or give a short talk, or give out prizes.
- Plan an event based on a competition such as the Olympics, World Cup or Wimbledon. Show the action live on a big screen. Hold some sort of decathlon, triathlon, football or tennis event.
- Hold a multi-sport event or a fun games event with no real sports at all, just crazy ones.
- Ask children to pair up with a parent or other adult to involve whole families and contribute to building parent-child relationships.

Bible Explorer

A slightly different sort of activity that individuals can undertake is to lead Bible Explorer courses in schools. This is not a sporting activity but is very much in line with learning through movement.

Bible Explorer is a children's version of *Walk Thru the Bible*, which was developed in 1976 by a Professor of

Theology for his students. Many people know sections of the Bible well but don't understand how it all fits together. *Walk Thru the Bible* uses Stephen's speech in Acts, which gives an overview of the entire Old Testament in 49 verses, as a basis and adds visual aids, mnemonics, drama, action and fun to help people to grasp the complete story. The teaching room is turned into a map of the Middle East and an instructor guides the group through over about six hours. I undertook a *Walk Thru the Bible* day several years ago and found it extremely helpful and fun to do. Actions were used throughout which greatly assisted the memorization process.

Bible Explorer is designed for groups of nine to eleven year olds in schools who may know almost nothing about the Bible. There are five sessions on the Old Testament and five on the New Testament. Hand signs, drama and puzzles are among the memory aids used.

Here is one teacher's comment: 'Brilliant, especially the full children's participation with all the actions. They participated well, retained the information and thoroughly enjoyed the work.'

In conclusion

If you reach out to the children in your community in one or more of these ways you will be praying that some of these children will become part of your regular children's ministry and that they and their families will become part of God's family and members of your church.

Due to the nature of these energetic outreach events you will no doubt attract lively children and you will certainly need to employ some of the methods outlined in the earlier chapters of this book in order to engage them in learning more about Jesus.

With those involved in sports teams you will need to take an interest in both their success and setbacks. With those who struggle with academic or behavioural difficulties at school you will need to be sensitive to their needs and try to ensure they find success in your sessions. With all the children you will need to have fun and build good relationships.

Having read this book I hope you see games, action and movement activities as an essential part of your children's work and have gained new ideas. I pray that you and your children will enjoy learning about Jesus together more than ever and that your input will help your church to be known as a dynamic, lively family, filled with God's life and love.

Appendix

Discussion Topics

Use these questions on your own, with a colleague, or during a children's workers' team meeting or training session.

1   In what way is God an active God? Find five passages that show how God has acted throughout history via nature and mankind. Try looking in Deuteronomy, Psalms and Isaiah.

2   What are the consequences for children's health and learning if they are denied adequate movement experiences? Do you know any children who show signs of having lacked movement experiences in earlier years? How might you help them?

3   What are the characteristics of bodily-kinesthetic learners? Can you identify any children with this learning style in your group?

4   Choose a Bible story that you will be covering shortly and make up actions that will help you to tell it and the children to remember it.

5   Plan an active follow-up game for the same story.

6   Choose another Bible story that you will soon be covering. Make up an age-appropriate game or physical challenge that reinforces the main theme you will be emphasizing when you tell this story.

7   Choose one or more of these verses and make up actions to aid memorization:

• Your word is a lamp to my feet and a light to my path. (Psalm 119:105)

• I have hidden your word in my heart that I might not sin against you. (Psalm119:11)

• There is neither Jew nor Greek, slave nor free, male nor female, for you are all one in Christ Jesus. (Galatians 3:28)

• How long will you waver between two opinions? If the Lord is God, follow him. (1 Kings 18:21)

• Let us not give up meeting together, as some are in the habit of doing, but let us encourage one another – and all the more as you see the day approaching. (Hebrews 10:25)

8   Make a list of action songs that you know. Learn some new songs (try the *12 New Children's Praise Songs* series from Children's Ministry) and make up actions.

9   How could your church use sport and games in outreach to local children and their families? Discuss the ideas in Chapter 7 and try to generate more of your own. Consider the needs of your community, facilities, equipment, personnel and budget.

10   Pray – for the children in your groups, for yourselves as leaders, for the implementation of new ideas that have resulted from your reading and discussion.

Safety Checklist

This list is particularly for active games and sports.

Be careful when tall or heavy children are mixed with small or light children. Depending on the activity, you may need separate groups that will not necessarily be based on age. Think about size and ability.

Some children may be embarrassed about their big or small size. Try to minimize this being an issue, e.g. think about the size of hoops they crawl through, the clothes they wear if they are 'dressing up', the categories you call out if sorting them into groups or orders.

Do you have enough space for the activity to be safe? Would it be sensible to walk instead of run if the area seems small?

Make sure everyone is aware of other players and what they are doing to avoid collisions.

Do children need to remove watches, rings, earrings, bracelets or other jewellery?

Are children wearing appropriate footwear? If not, do not suggest bare feet or socks as they may slip or get trodden on by other children. Find a suitable helping role for them.

If children are unable to participate for any reason, try to involve them in timing, counting, helping others, being a 'team captain', cheering, etc.

Have an arranged signal that will stop the activity quickly if necessary, for example, a whistle blast.

Check any equipment that you are using to make sure it is not broken or unsafe in any way.

If you are using a ball indoors, either make sure it is soft enough so that it will not break any windows or cause other damage, or ensure windows etc. are protected so that the correct ball for the sport can be used.

Do not go straight into a strenuous activity without warming up first. Allow at least five minutes for some easy walking, jogging, and mobility.

Outside, avoid areas where traffic or dogs could be a danger. Check the area for dangerous objects.

Insist upon a positive, encouraging attitude at all times, i.e. no laughing or groaning at others' attempts.

If doing 'trust' activities, where children have to rely on others, stop the activity immediately if you see signs of 'messing about'.

If using any type of instructor for a specialist activity, e.g. for sports coaching or outdoor pursuits, ask them about their qualifications and insurance cover. You can check National Governing Body web sites to see the required level of instructor qualification for the activity your children will be undertaking.

It is advisable to have someone with a First Aid qualification present.

Discipline Checklist

Set ground rules before you start. You should have general rules agreed with any group of children with whom you work, but you may need additional rules for active games and sports.

Plan carefully. Have everything ready before the children arrive. Make sure you know how long you will spend on each activity and what the children will move on to next.

Have at least one leader to lead the children and another to look out for problems.

Masking tape on the floor can help to define playing areas and contain children waiting for their turn.

A yellow (warning) and red ('sent off' or banned for the next session) card system can be useful.

Put the children into teams and use points and prizes to encourage enthusiasm and good behaviour.

See also the *Children's Ministry Guide to Dealing with Disruptive Children* by Andy Back.

Further Reading

- Alliston, Ruth. *Children's Ministry Guide to Using Dance and Drama*. Kingsway Communications Ltd, UK, 2002.
- Back, Andy. *Children's Ministry Guide to Dealing with Disruptive Children*. Kingsway Communications Ltd, UK, 2002.
- Cheatum, Billye Ann, and Hammond, Allison A. *Physical Activities for Improving Children's Learning and Behaviour: A Guide to Sensory Motor Development*. Human Kinetics, USA, 2000.
- Clouder, Christopher, Jenkinson, Sally, and Large, Martin. *The Future of Childhood*. Hawthorne Press, UK, 2000.
- Coakley, Jay. *Sport in Contemporary Society: Issues and Controversies,* Seventh Edition, McGraw Hill, USA, 2001.
- Hannaford, Carla. *Smart Moves: Why learning is not all in your head*. Great Ocean Publishers, Arlington, Virginia, USA, 1995.
- Jensen, Eric. *Learning with the Body in Mind – The Scientific Basis for Energizers, Movement, Play, Games, and Physical Education*. The Brain Store, Inc., San Diego, CA, USA, 2000.

- LeFever, Marlene. *Learning Styles: Reaching everyone God gave you to teach*. Kingsway Publications, UK, 1998.
- Price, Sue. *Children's Ministry Guide to Tailored Teaching for 5-9s*. Kingsway Communications Ltd, UK, 2002.
- Weir, Stuart. *What the Book says about Sport*. Bible Reading Fellowship, 2000.

Web sites

- Bible Explorer: www.Bible.org.uk
- British Heart Foundation: www.bhf.org.uk
- Christians in Sport: www.christiansinsport.org.uk
- Kids Games: www.thekidsgames.com
- Sports equipment: www.newitts.com
- Sportz Klub: www.sportzklub.co.uk